YOU'RE
NOT
A HELPLESS
VICTIM

YOU'RE NOT A HELPLESS VICTIM

Take Control of Your Life and Don't Allow Yourself to Become a Miserable F*ck

PAUL DEBIASE

You're Not a Helpless Victim: Take Control of Your Life and Don't Allow Yourself to Become a Miserable F*ck

Published by Gatekeeper Press
7853 Gunn Hwy., Suite 209
Tampa, FL 33626
www.GatekeeperPress.com

ISBN (paperback): 9781662937156

DEDICATION

I am dedicating this book to my daughters Gabriella and Claudia. They are off to college now. As their dad, I am feeling like I probably should have spent more time talking with them about some of the more important lessons that I have learned. I sort of just took a "wing-it" approach to fatherhood, and I now wish that I had a few more sit-downs with them. Actually, I don't recall ever having had a single sit-down with them, and I never really came out and verbally expressed my beliefs, values, or morals. I just sort of assumed that they knew where I stood and that they would learn as they observed. I also wanted them to form their own identities without excessive influence from me or other adult figures. Yet, I do want to share with them what I have learned, and they are free to absorb or dismiss as much as they desire. So, here is what I have learned and what I think is important. I am not going to take credit for all of what follows, as some of it comes from others; but I have been able to put the various lessons to use and can give a firsthand account as to their truthfulness and usefulness.

INTRODUCTION

Let's keep this intro short and sweet.

I am writing this book to tell you and remind you to *take control of your life*. That's right, it is your life, so for crying out loud, take control of it.

You are not a helpless victim. Your emotional state of mind should not be at the mercy of others. It's your emotional state of mind, so *own it*. Take control of your life, your surroundings, your feelings, everything.

It's not uncommon for us to have setbacks and to feel like things aren't going our way. We just need a reminder from time to time that we are capable of controlling our state of mind.

If/when you are ready to take control, you can use this book to help guide you.

That's it.

Are you ready to take control of own your life?

If so, read on. What follows are a few lessons I have learned.

CONTENTS

SMILE

Yes, this lesson is that simple: *Smile*.

Go ahead, if you're not smiling right now, then smile. Raise those cheeks up nice and high. Higher. C'mon, put a huge smile on your face. Hold it. Keep holding it. Notice anything?

We have been trained to think that the connection between our feelings, our emotions, and our expressions are an inside-out relationship. In other words, how we feel *inside* manifests itself on the *outside*, through our facial expressions and emotions. There is a lot of truth to that. If you're feeling shitty inside, you probably have a bad look on your face. If you're feeling happy inside, then you have a smile on your face. So, whatever we have going on *inside* of us dictates how we look on the *outside*.

But the opposite can be equally true. Yes, we can control how we feel inside by how we project on the outside. In other words, you can make yourself feel good inside by simply putting a smile on your face. Imagine that—first you smile, then you feel good inside. It works and it's easy.

So, that is the lesson. Don't wait to be happy before you put a smile on your face. Make a point of smiling first, and let those feelings of happiness come in.

Smiling and having that good feeling inside is also contagious. On a daily basis, we interact with all sorts of people, from family members to friends to complete strangers. Try to make a point of making your first visible expression a smile. This will almost always be reciprocated with a smile back. This is particularly true when encountering a perfect stranger. It happens to me all of the time as I run or walk through the neighborhood. Our subdivision has had an influx of Indian and Muslim immigrants, many of whom are elderly. You can tell that they probably don't speak or understand English. It is kind of apparent that they are fine if we just pass each other up, not even acknowledging each other's presence. But at that very moment when our paths meet, I make a point of smiling at them and sometimes include a "good morning." Guess what? They smile back and I can tell that at that moment where we are smiling at each other, we both feel better for having that exchange. It didn't take much. It was kind of simple. It makes me feel better inside for having done it.

I would imagine that the same can be said about laughing, but I am not going to ask you to laugh right now as there might be people around and that would be weird if you just randomly broke out laughing. But try and laugh as much as possible; it's better than crying.

So think about it . . . of all the emotions that we would want inside of us, I would imagine that happiness is the one that we would strive for most often. If achieving that feeling is as easy as smiling, then doesn't it make sense to smile as much as possible?

Sidenote: when I smile at someone and they don't smile back, it really pisses me off. (Motherfucker can't smile back?????)

BAD NEWS

We have a way of characterizing everything that happens to us as "good" or "bad" and then allowing that characterization to dictate how we feel for the remainder of the day, the next week, the next month, year, and so on. Well, I suppose that if everything that happens to us can be characterized as "good news," then no problem. But, we all experience setbacks:

- You didn't get the job or didn't get the promotion.
- You didn't make the team.
- He/she chose someone else.
- You're not making as much money.
- You're not able to do the things you used to do.

I think you get the point. We are all bound to have setbacks, and I think it is only normal that we feel a certain amount of disappointment, frustration, jealousy, and resentment when things don't seem to go the way we wanted. Indeed, we probably invested a lot of time and resources to achieve something that at that moment in time is important to us.

The lesson is this—When you receive "bad news," do *not* allow those feelings of disappointment, frustration, jealousy, and resentment to linger *because*:

Today's "bad news" has a way of becoming tomorrow's "good news."

Almost all bad news seems to have a silver lining. It's just that the silver lining may not immediately manifest itself. Indeed, for certain events, it could take a while before you figure out that what you originally perceived to be "bad" was actually a blessing. Look back at every example above. When those events first happen, they appear to be devastating; but look at how each event can turn into a blessing:

- **You didn't get the job or promotion**: You later find out that the job or promotion which you so desperately wanted absolutely sucks. And the person who got the job or promotion instead of you is absolutely miserable, or worse, that the position has now been terminated, and the person who landed the "dream" job is out of work.
- **You didn't make the team**: That allowed you to switch sports or join a different team, and you have made many new friends because of it.
- **He or she chose someone else**: You later found someone much better, and you would never have met the "new" guy or girl had the jackass chosen you.

- **You're not making as much money**: You're not wasting as much money anymore.
- **You're not able to do the things you used to do**: You have found new things to do, which are just as rewarding.

So you see, when the "bad news" arrives, *do not* allow the feelings of disappointment, jealousy, frustration, and resentment to consume you. Instead, start to think "there must be a reason why this happened" and "one day I'll look back and see this same event as a blessing."

I can give you a few firsthand examples:

#1: I attended a top-ten law school (Northwestern), and that was a "golden ticket" or a "guarantee" that upon graduating I would have my pick of jobs at almost any of the most prestigious law firms and/or companies anywhere in the country and at a starting salary of $125,000 (1992). Indeed, during my first two years, all the big firms and companies flew in from all over the country to our school to recruit us. I envisioned working in a great downtown office building, having an awesome office, great lunches, dinners, social events, etc. That is what was promised to us, and that is what we expected. Well, in my final year and right before graduation, the economy tanked and we were in a deep recession. Bad news, law firms were not hiring. It sucked. No "dream job." No "second choice" or "third choice" job either. I took a job working for a two-person law firm for $35,000 (less money than I was making when

I worked as a construction laborer during my summer jobs.) After six months, I was told that they couldn't keep me anymore. *Wow.* I was upset and felt cheated. Let me fast forward a bit. I started my own practice with no clients and put a desk, chair, and phone in my dad's travel agency/bookkeeping office. I made $26,000 my first year while living with my parents. Slowly and steadily my practice grew. I developed a great reputation and built many relationships with great clients. When the big firms started hiring again, I decided to stay put. I never worked for anyone else again. I must tell you that being self-employed is awesome. No boss to answer to. No office politics. My law school friends who eventually landed the dream jobs tell me horror stories of working at the big, prestigious firms. Man, oh man, am I ever grateful for the "bad news" that arrived in 1992.

#2: The kids are in soccer tryouts. We have invested a lot of money and time and have expectations and desires for them to make the Travel "A" team. You guessed it, "bad news" and with it feelings of resentment, jealousy, disappointment. It felt like we were "robbed" of something that was ours. Well, the kids made the "B" or even "C" team, and guess what, they were the stars of the team and they got the most playing time and their self-confidence was sky high. When we would talk to friends whose kids had made the "A" team, we heard stories about limited playing time, how serious it all was, and injuries. Yep, the "bad news" turned out to be a blessing.

Now, the flip side is also true. Today's "good news" can be tomorrow's "bad news."

Look, when the good news arrives, allow yourself to enjoy the moment, feel satisfaction, achievement, and glory. You probably put in a lot of time and effort to achieve something that, at a given moment, is important to you. You have to allow yourself to *enjoy* these moments. You just have to know not to gloat and not become comfortable with today's achievements. Just look at the same list set forth above, and how with the passage of time they can later become "bad news":

- **You got the job or promotion**: turns out that the job/promotion that you so desperately wanted, sucks.
- **You made the team**: turns out that the team contains a bunch of assholes, and you are now stuck with this smelly group.
- **He chose *you***: turns out that he's not such a prize.
- **You're rolling in the dough $$$**: This allows you to develop and sustain horrible spending habits and forces you to become a slave to money.

So yes, enjoy the "good news," and allow yourself to experience all of the wonderful feelings of satisfaction, achievement, and glory that come with it. But don't do so at the expense of others' feelings and do not become too comfortable living within today's "good news." Start creating opportunities for more and different and even better "good news."

Again, the lesson is that when "bad news" arrives, realize that it is temporary and don't allow those feelings of disappointment, resentment, and jealousy to consume you. Odds are you will look back and see the same events as a blessing. (Unless, of course, you place an order at the drive-through and assume they got it right and drive off; you get home, open the bag, and "bad news," it's the wrong order—they gave you the cheese dog instead of the cheeseburger that you were craving. No silver lining here. Sorry, this can't turn into good news—just eat the damn cheese dog, and read the next chapter.)

STOP COMPLAINING AND STOP THE "BLAME GAME"

I'm not sure why, but many of us have developed a habit of complaining and blaming others. Like, somehow, we are always victims of fate or we are being victimized by others. I suppose that many of us don't even realize how much of our time we devote to complaining. Just take a look back at your day, or the last few days, and make a list of stuff that you have been complaining about:

- I have the flu and it sucks.
- I am so tired.
- It's too hot in this house.
- I am not busy at work.
- Traffic is so bad.
- The service and food at the restaurant sucked.

That's a lot of negative energy. Complain, complain, complain. All that really does is allow you to characterize yourself as a hopeless victim at the mercy of others or of circumstances outside of our control. Really? Come on.

Maybe you should look within yourself to see if somehow, and in some way, you are responsible for whatever it is that you are complaining about. Or, rather, work on the resolution. You're not a helpless victim. Take control to resolve things. Don't be that person that constantly spews out complaints or blames others. Be the person who identifies problems and then works toward their solutions.

The lesson here is to not allow yourself to play the part of a helpless victim. Rather, take responsibility for whatever it is that you are complaining about. Don't blame others. You put yourself in that situation. Own it. Learn from it.

- So yes, I have the flu and I am pretty sure who gave it to me . . . but I am responsible for allowing those germs to spread to me, and next time I'll do more to make sure I don't get sick.
- Yes, it's too hot in this house but I am capable of solving this, aren't I? Rather than complain about it, let me get my ass off this couch and open a window or something, other than complaining.
- Yes, traffic is bad but maybe I'll try and leave a bit earlier next time.
- Yes, I am constantly tired but I am doing too much and need to cut back.
- Yes, things are slow at work but I haven't really done much to drum up business, and I am capable of generating more business or going in a different direction.

- Yes, the food at this restaurant sucked but, guess what, I picked the restaurant—I know not to come back.

So, you see how every complaint needs to follow with some sort of an admission that you have contributed to the situation that you are complaining about, and you are capable of overcoming the situation. *Don't just complain. You're not a helpless victim. Don't seek pity. Solve the fucking problem and get over it already.*

- *Complaining and blaming others = negative energy.*
- *Solving problems = positive energy.*

HELPING OTHERS AND GIVING

This one seems really easy at first glance and usually it is:

Whenever possible, give and help others.

Many self-help books and articles have explained how the act of giving has two beneficiaries. The recipient obviously benefits. But the person who is doing the giving actually benefits as well. There is a certain amount of "feel-good" emotion that we derive when we give and help others. So, if this seemed simple and easy a minute ago, it would certainly seem easier now. It's a win-win—help others and we have two winners. Pretty simple and straightforward, right? What's the next chapter about? Hold on.

Question: Are there times when the act of helping others actually hurts them? I think you see where I am going with this. Sometimes, helping others and giving isn't so simple.

When it comes to strangers and "public causes," I think that the act of giving is easy and simple. You can give and move on. The recipient will benefit. You feel good. Done. Take the Red Cross or the panhandler as examples. They clearly need help. You have some spare cash. You give. They benefit. You feel good. Easy. Move along.

With family and good friends, it is more complicated. *You have to put some thought into it before giving.* When we are asked to give and help this group, this is where we cannot just give and help mindlessly. There are times when a family member or friend will be in need of assistance. They may ask for help or they may not. We will feel compelled to help out. The point is this: put some thought into your upcoming benevolence. The easiest solution is probably not the best solution. Don't give/help to make yourself feel good that you have "come to the rescue." Don't just write the check and call it a day.

There are many examples:

- Debbie needs financial assistance, again.
- Frankie needs to get bailed out of jail for the third time this month.
- Tommy is out of work.
- Suzy can't afford to come with us this vacation.

In each example we can "come to the rescue" and feel good about ourselves. But, we should have invested the time to get to the root of the problems. Here, helping and giving mindlessly can ultimately hurt the recipient.

Once you get to the root of the problem, now comes the hard part. You see, sometimes it's best not to help. There are times when less is more. Or perhaps it's best to help with some structure. The point is to give it some thought so that you don't become the enabler. *Don't become the enabler.*

I've seen this "giving" and "lack of giving" dynamic play out with the superrich. I'm talking about the likes of Bill Gates and Warren Buffet. When it comes to strangers and public causes, they are very generous. They have established foundations that will give to the needy (strangers) and to public causes. However, when it comes to their families, they have very publicly told their family and friends that very little will be left to them. These individuals recognize how "helping" their children with an inheritance of billions of dollars would most likely turn their children into worthless members of society. You have to applaud them for having the guts to make their own family members struggle for themselves. You see, they are not giving mindlessly. They thought things through. They want what is best for their children and have determined that a few billion dollars head start could actually be a bad thing. It would be interesting to follow these kids and then compare them to other kids whose parents took the easy road.

Okay, so as a wrap up.

Yes, give and help others. It will make you feel better about yourself, and your recipient will hopefully appreciate it at a certain level.

When dealing with family and friends, give some thought before giving/helping mindlessly. Have a plan that will tackle the underlying problem. This may involve *not* helping at a moment's notice. Indeed:

- Debbie might have to make things work within her budget.
- Maybe it's best for Frankie to spend a few nights in the pokey.
- Don't be so fast to find Tommy a job at your buddy's business.
- Don't pay for Suzy to come on this trip, as this may cause her to learn better saving habits.

You see, sometimes "coming to the rescue" is the easy thing to do but the wrong thing to do. Certainly, it is difficult to watch a family member or friend struggle. But if you simply "come to the rescue" without putting any thought into it, recognize that you are basically saying that you don't want to invest the time needed to truly help.

BE PROACTIVE, NOT REACTIVE

A reactive person allows the actions or inactions of others to dictate how he/she will then act. Reactive people are always looking to strike back. They allow themselves to lower their set of values to match the values of others.

A proactive person lives their life based upon a core set of values and principles and does not allow the actions/inactions of others to dictate how they will act.

Hypothetical Situation #1: You're part of an extensive friend group, and Debbie has assumed the role of organizing an event. You come to learn that Debbie has not included you in the event. What do you do?

Hypothetical situation #2: You have come to learn that Suzie is talking bad about you. What are you going to do?

Hypothetical situation #3: You just lost your tennis match. Your opponent has proven to be a poor sport and has begun a series of chants. What are you going to do?

Hypothetical situation #4: You have been trying to reach a friend. They fail to answer your repeated messages. No return call. No return texts. What are you going to do?

In each hypothetical situation, it is pretty much assumed that how others act will dictate how you will react. It doesn't have to be that way. Indeed, it should *not* be that way. *How others act defines who they are.* Now it's your turn to bat.

The person who is proactive lives their life based upon their core values. This person is extremely confident. This person has a very defined set of principles that guide their behavior. They are not waiting on others' behavior to influence how they will act in any given moment. What others decide to do is their own business and will not sway the proactive person's behavior.

The person who is reactive lives their life constantly reacting to others' behavior and/or some other external stimuli. They are insecure. This person lacks a core set of principles and is capable of a wide range of behavior. How others act will define their own behavior.

A proactive person will have a very defined set of values:

- They don't lie.
- They work hard.
- They don't engage in drama.
- They help others.

Let's look back at our hypothetical situations and see how a proactive vs. a reactive person will handle each situation.

Hypothetical #1: Debbie didn't invite you.

- Reactive person: purposefully plan an event and don't invite Debbie—and this back-and-forth will then repeat itself and will make other guests uncomfortable when organizing other events.
- Proactive person: be sure to invite Debbie, which will show her and others that you are capable of hosting all sorts. Drama is over.

Hypothetical #2: Suzie is talking badly about you.

- Reactive person: Reciprocate with some dirt on Suzie. This will escalate and continue, drama continues . . . take four.
- Proactive person: be sure to point out one of Suzie's positive qualities. This will diffuse the nasty dialogue and will show Suzie and others that you don't engage in name calling.

Hypothetical #3: Your opponent is being a bad sport.

- Reactive person: "I'll stick that tennis racket up your ass." This will lead to more banter, so if it's more banter that you want then keep reacting and keep lowering yourself.
- Proactive person: "Thanks for the tennis match; I had lots of fun and it was a great workout." This will shut him up. So, if you want to end the banter, rise above him.

Hypothetical #4: Your friend isn't answering your calls.

- Reactive person: Will stop trying to reach the friend, or worse, will reciprocate and not answer when he finally gets around to calling back. This can go on for days, weeks, months, or years, to see who will give in first.
- Proactive person: Keep trying to reach him. If/when he does call, jump all over it. Communication is flowing and that is what was originally desired.

The life lesson is this—*Have a well-established core set of values and principles that will guide your behavior!!!!* How others act is irrelevant, as you will not allow their actions or inactions to define who you are as a person.

Live your life according to your values.

It really pisses people off when you don't lower yourself to their miserable existence. Rise above their misery.

You see, what you are basically telling people is this:

You can steal from me; you can lie to me; you can call me names; you can make fun of me, and all of those things that you have done *define who you are as a person*—and I am not going to lower myself to your level. I have a different set of values that guide me. *Boom, motherfucker!!!!!!*

YOU HAVE TO BE CONFRONTATIONAL SOMETIMES—DON'T ALLOW YOURSELF TO LIVE IN RESENTMENT

Resentment:

- The feeling of bitterness for having been treated unfairly.
- The feeling of persistent ill will at someone for something regarded as a wrong, insult, or injury.

It is inevitable that:

- You will be lied to.
- You will be misled.
- You will be treated unfairly.
- You will be betrayed.
- You will be taken advantage of.

- You will not be appreciated for something that you have done.
- You will be insulted.

(Hopefully not all on the same day.)

What are you going to do? As you can see from the definition, resentment is a "feeling" that we have inside of us—and not a good one. But the key is that it is a feeling that we have and presumably should have.

I'll make this short and sweet. (I've written and re-written this chapter a few times now and it went off in different directions, but I think I've got it now.)

If and when any of the above happens, you have to immediately deal with the situation at hand. *You have to confront the situation right then and there!!!!* Far too often, we are afraid to be confrontational. Not immediately taking action is the *easy* thing to do.

- We sense that we are being taken advantage of, yet we fail to act.
- We sense that we are being lied to, but we fail to address it.
- We feel unappreciated, but we fail to state it.
- We feel insulted, but we fail to let that be known.

Failing to immediately confront the situation is what leads to resentment and, therefore, you are partially to blame if/when you have feelings of resentment. Sure, she lied to you and for that she is to blame. But your inability to immediately confront the situation will allow this incident to simmer for hours, weeks, months, or years. If only you had the guts to have confronted the situation immediately, this could have been dealt with a long time ago.

Force people to be accountable for their actions and statements. Will this be uncomfortable? Oh yeah. Will you be rocking the boat? Yep.

The alternative is to keep quiet and live in a sea of resentment—what a miserable existence.

The lesson is simple: Confront and deal with situations before they lead to resentment. Have the guts to confront matters before they lead to years of resentment. *Stand up for yourself. Confront the situation immediately.*

If you find yourself living in a world of resentment, know that you bear some responsibility. Sure, the person who took advantage of you is mostly to blame; but your current state of emotions is your responsibility, and your failure to confront a matter has now led to this. Stop being a miserable fuck and deal with the situation. You're not a helpless victim in this.

It takes a lot of energy to be mad at someone. That energy could be and should be used more productively (not sure how or where to fit this in, but there it is).

BIG DECISIONS

I urge you first to learn to put *small* decisions in their proper perspective.

Let's look at some decisions that we have to make on a daily basis:

- What should I wear?
- Where should we go eat?
- Should I take the expressway or local roads?
- Should I book that ticket now or wait for prices to go down?
- What kind of phone or car should I purchase?

Please learn to identify these decisions as trivial matters, as that is exactly what they are: trivial matters. If and when you find yourself stressing about these types of decisions for any length of time, recognize that you have failed to keep things in their proper perspective.

You need to treat these everyday decisions as inconsequential. They really have no consequence on your well-being so, again, if you feel any stress, you have failed to keep things in perspective. It wouldn't surprise me if 80–90% of all decisions we make fall into this category, so most of the time our decision-making attitude should be: get the facts, make a decision, and move on. Sure, you may not get it right but at the end of the day, you will still be okay with mistakenly having chosen the wrong outfit, the wrong restaurant, or the wrong phone. You'll be okay, so please get over it already.

Well, the chapter is titled "Big Decisions" so, unfortunately, we aren't going to be able to go through life treating all decisions as inconsequential. Some decisions have enormous consequences.

Let's look at some *big decisions*:

- Should I accept that job?
- Should I marry that person?
- Should I relocate?

Wow. Wow. Wow. The consequences of these decisions appear enormous, and at a certain level they most certainly are.

I am here to tell you and teach you that even the *big decisions* can be somewhat inconsequential, as long as you get one decision correct. Yes, there is one decision that you have to make, which is the mother of all other decisions, and if you get that one singular decision correct, all other decisions are somewhat inconsequential.

So, what is the mother of all decisions?

Decide on who you want to be as a person. Decide on what you want your identity to be.

Hopefully, you have decided to be a solid individual, one who is committed to being truthful, helping others, working hard, one who refrains from gossip and avoids drama, one who is committed to new experiences and having fun, one who is devoted to meaningful causes.

If your decision is that you want to become rich, or if you have chosen to be identified by your occupation, your marital status, your location, then all of the other decisions that have to be made become more stressful, as they impact who you want to be as a person.

If your decision is that you want to be a solid individual, then all other decisions have much less of an impact because at the end of the day, you have already made a bigger decision and you got it right!!!!!!!!

That is the biggest decision you have to make!!! Who are you? What is your identity?

If/when you have a big decision to make, remind yourself that there is actually a bigger decision that needs to be made. If you are confident that you got the bigger decision correct, then suddenly the big decision in front of you isn't as important.

So, if you end up accepting the wrong job, marrying the wrong person, living in the wrong area, you will still be okay, as you have yourself to fall back on.

Once you have decided to be a solid individual, all other decisions, big and small, are somewhat inconsequential.

ALCOHOL

I have written and re-written this chapter a few times now. I know the point that I want to make, but its taking me way too long to get there so I'll cut to the chase and say what I want to say up front.

Alcohol limits your potential to accomplish more things in life.

There it is. That's the point that I want to make. I suppose the lesson is for you to be aware of that and just remember that.

Notice that this is just a statement that I want you to be aware of and to remember. I am not saying, "and therefore stop drinking."

You see, you might end up like me—a social drinker. Okay, let's say more than a social drinker but never to the point where I let alcohol interfere with my roles as a husband, father, friend, head of household, etc. I naturally assumed that alcohol was never a "problem" in my life and I'll go on saying that it hasn't been a "problem." But what

I have come to learn is that there should be two questions being asked:

1. Is alcohol causing any problems with my roles as a husband, father, friend, head of household, etc.? Answer: *No.*

2. Has alcohol limited my potential to accomplish more things in life? Answer: *Probably.*

Look, if the goal in life is to try and accomplish as many things as is humanly possible, then alcohol is a problem. If you ever find yourself thinking that you could be or should be doing more, then cut out the booze.

This chapter isn't written for the casual drinker. You know, the person who has a few drinks while out to dinner with friends and then doesn't think about alcohol or having a drink until the next "right occasion" presents itself, which may not be until the following week or even longer. If this describes you, awesome. You seem to have found a way to have fun without the added stimulus.

This chapter also isn't for the problematic drinker. You know, the one who has allowed alcohol to interfere with their relationships, employment, etc. If your alcohol consumption ever interferes with your relationship with your spouse or kids, gets in the way of your job performance, or causes you physical harm beyond bad hangovers . . . it's probably time to stop. If this describes you, I am truly sorry because you are consuming alcohol to hide or mask some other underlying issues.

This chapter is meant for the person who uses alcohol just short of becoming a problematic drinker. This person feels like: (1) anything that is deemed "not fun" in life can be easily turned into "fun" with a six-pack (cutting the grass sucks, but have a few beers along the way and now it's not so bad) and (2) anything already deemed "fun" in life can be a hell of a lot more fun with a six-pack or two being consumed along with it. I think you get my drift. Let's just say a person drinks to have fun, and they like to have a lot of fun. Let's call this person a "social drinker."

The "social drinker" is a solid member of society with many positive qualities:

- Great partner and parent
- Great job
- Nice house
- Financially solid
- Physically fit
- Charitable

I am spending a lot of time describing this "social drinker," as it might describe a great many people. Indeed, I fit this characterization and have never thought much about my alcohol consumption until I learned the lesson of this chapter.

You see, the "social drinker" has achieved many accomplishments and hasn't allowed alcohol consumption to interfere with everything they have accomplished, and it hasn't interfered with their other responsibilities.

So, what's the problem? What's the lesson? Why write a chapter on this subject?

The lesson is this: Yes, the "social drinker" has many achievements and accomplishments. He is a good father. He is a good husband. He has more than adequately provided for his family. He has given back in some form or another. BUT HE COULD HAVE ACHIEVED MORE. HE COULD HAVE BEEN EVEN BETTER at each and every thing. It's kind of simple. Once you start drinking, you are limiting yourself.

Look, I'm not here to preach abstinence. That would be very hypocritical of me. It's just important that you realize alcohol is limiting some other things that you can be accomplishing.

Looking back, I sometimes wonder: *Did alcohol prevent me from accomplishing more?* Probably. Do I resent it??? I don't think so. Actually, I'll go all the way to "no"—I don't resent it.

Here is where I think I failed, and perhaps you can do better: As a society, we start drinking way too early in life— early teens for most. That's when I started, and that's what I observe in the next generation. So the cycle has repeated itself. My failure is that I didn't come up with any better alternatives. Maybe if you are more conscious of this cycle, you can think of better alternatives. Kids should be allowed to remain kids as long as possible.

This chapter was exhausting, and I can't wait to write about something else.

RULES

I get it. Without rules, there is chaos and that is no good. Just take a look at some third-world countries or even some more advanced societies that live with little or no rules. Chaos. It sucks. Everybody just sort of doing things the way that they want. The lack of order leads to gridlock and stagnation. While everyone does what is in their own best interest, the society fails to advance, because nobody is acting for the good of the masses.

I guess that as humans we need direction. We need constraint. We need order. We need rules for us to follow so that we can have a working society.

So we have many, many rules. Some are imposed by governmental bodies, others are imposed by our religion. Then our parents want to get in on the fun: soon we have the teachers, homeowner associations, businesses that we frequent, clubs that we join. The list goes on and on. Lots of rules. Lots of other people and groups wanting to control our behavior.

Well, apart from my intro wherein I recognize the need for rules so that we can have a functioning society,

I have to say I am not a big fan. I actually despise all the rules and hate the people who try to enforce them. I can't stand being told what I can do, what I can't do, when I can do something, how I have to dress, when I have to do something, how often I have to do something, when I have to attend—enough!!!!!

Look, most rules start with good intentions. It's just that, many times, after a rule is written and imposed, it may not solve the problem that it was supposed to fix and may even cause a greater problem. Let's look at speed limits. Certainly, we can all appreciate the intention of these rules. Without speed limits, people would drive at speeds that would pose a danger to themselves and others. The solution: Impose speed limits. The problem comes when politicians set arbitrary limits without any notions as to practical applications. We live in a metropolitan area where the speed limit on the expressway is 55 mph. Why 55 mph??? Oh, I am sure that there is some study that lawmakers can point to. But why not be practical. Have they ever tried to drive 55 mph on the expressway???? I can tell you that even if you are in the right-hand lane driving 55 mph, you are *way more* of a danger to yourself and to others than the guy going seventy keeping up with traffic. So as you can see, the intent of the rule is good. But if it's a poorly written rule, then it may cause more harm than the problem it sought to cure.

I am not advocating civil disobedience. It's just that many people in our society make it their lifelong mission to impose and enforce rules that somehow advance their own individual plans. The rules that were supposed to be put in place to somehow benefit society as a whole have been written and enforced by a few who are trying to push their own agenda. These rule makers may be career politicians who want to decide for the rest of us when and how high we should jump. Fuck them.

Here's my take on it: Figure out what the intent of the rule is. Follow the intent of the rule (excess speed on expressways can have bad consequences, so avoid excess speed.) The rule itself (55 mph) is just a bunch of details thought up by another human. So, if you find the rule to be arbitrary and stupid, then implement your own rule that is consistent with the intent of the rule (I'll go 70 mph and keep up with traffic, so we are all safe.)

Be prepared to get into some trouble: Pay the fine, pay the penalty. That's okay. You see, I'd rather live my life according to my rules than to be somebody's bitch all the time. I'll take my punishment and be content in knowing that I didn't allow myself to be a blind follower.

Oh yeah, the rule I hate the most: dress codes at restaurants. I get it. The intent of the rule is to keep people from coming in looking like slobs. This would make other patrons feel uncomfortable or may even ruin the other patrons' experience. So, in keeping with the intent of the rule, don't wear shoes that have your toes sticking out, put on a clean shirt that doesn't smell, make yourself look respectable. Now go in there and enjoy yourself, right?

Hold on, they are saying that you need to wear slacks, even though it's eighty degrees. And, oh yeah, they are saying that they want you to wear a collared shirt and, oh yeah, they want you to wear a jacket or sport coat! Really???? What about a tie—do you want me to put on a fucking tie for you? How about some dress shoes? Oh, what about a watch. Maybe we should specify only a certain brand of watch. God forbid someone walks in wearing a Seiko.

What is this? A funeral? I want to have a good time and enjoy a good meal. It's not a fashion show. You see what happened. The intent of the rule is understandable. Then, somebody fails to consider any practical implications and pushes their agenda. Fuck them. I'll eat at a Burger King before I sit my ass in one of those jacket-wearing, pipe-smoking, Gucci-loving places. Fuck those people and their fucking restaurant.

Again, when confronted with a rule, try to understand the intent of the rule and adhere to the intent more than the rule itself. There is a good chance that the guy who wrote the rule may not have considered any practical implications and may be in the minority and/or is trying to push his own agenda. Fuck him.

LIFE IS . . .

Two theories here:

Theory #1: Life is a struggle for survival so prepare yourself accordingly. *Do whatever it takes to finish at the top.* The goal is to finish ahead of others. To do so, you must constantly prepare yourself. Life is a series of challenges and opportunities to succeed. Success is achieved by advancing yourself and finishing at the top in all facets of life. Happiness is derived by your success.

- Academically: Aim to finish at the top of your class. Take the classes that will challenge you and prepare you for the next chapter of your life. Take the teachers who are known to challenge their students. Do the extra credit. Take the exam prep tutor/class.
- Athletics: Aim to be the top player on the top team. Put in extra practice time.
- Work: Aim to impress and advance. Put in the extra time. Let it be known that you are capable and willing to do what it takes.

You see, in life there are winners and there are losers. Prepare yourself to be a winner. Happiness will follow. If you don't take the initiative to advance yourself, others will. If at first attempt you don't succeed, try again . . . and again . . . and again. Don't settle for mediocrity. The ramifications of not finishing at the top are unknown, so don't go there. Sure, others may find happiness at lower echelons, but they are really just making excuses for not having put in the time and effort to finish at the top.

Theory #2: Life is about achieving happiness regardless of your circumstances and standing among others. *Do your best and be happy.* The goal here is to find happiness no matter your circumstances. Absolutely, you must put forth the energy to do your best, but ultimately, finishing at the top is not the goal. Knowing that you did your best is good enough, no matter where you finish. Success is achieved by knowing that you did your best. Happiness can be found at all levels regardless of the outcome. You see, success is not defined by wins and losses. There can be winners and winners.

Analysis: So, which is it? I think we can all agree on this: life is meant to be enjoyed (see chapter titled "Have Fun.") My random thoughts on this:

- I tend to think that it's a lot easier to enjoy life while finishing on top.
- I do believe that success breeds happiness.

- I think that there is a danger to subscribing to theory #2, in that you can allow yourself to make excuses for failure.
- At its core, life is most definitely a struggle for survival. At a certain point, you will have to put in the time and effort to survive. If you subscribe to theory #1, you will put the time and effort at the beginning. You will survive. Happiness should follow. In theory #2, you will be happy but may not survive. I'm just not sure how you can be happy if you are struggling to survive????
- Theory #2 is looking more and more like a cop-out. Who knows, maybe theory #2 didn't even exist until they started handing out "participation" trophies.

Wow, it's theory #1 in a landslide. Theory #2 is for losers. If you don't finish on top, try again. Keep trying. Don't settle.

BEING "NICE"

The saying goes: "Nice guys finish last."

What does that mean? That those of us who have made a conscientious decision to live our lives by a decent set of values are a bunch of schmucks destined to be losers. I don't think that is the intended meaning. Nor do I think that it is meant to discourage all of us from being stand-up, solid citizens.

Let's take a better look at the "nice guy" (go ahead and substitute "girl," if you feel the need.)

- He is polite.
- He is considerate of others' feelings.
- He wants to be friends.
- He doesn't want to make waves.
- He wants us to get along.
- He wants to make things easy for the rest of us.
- He cares about our feelings.
- He is very accommodating.
- He doesn't want drama.

There you have it. The nice guy. I suppose if we would all strive to achieve the virtues of the "nice guy," the world would be a better place.

The questions are:

- Is there ever a time when it's not a good idea to be the nice guy?
- Is it okay to drop the "nice-guy" persona from time to time?
- Is it ever okay to be a prick? A jerk? A bitch?
- Are there times when being the "nice guy" will lead us to finish last?

The answer to all of the above questions is "yes."

The life lesson is this: In those instances, and roles where you are put in a position of leadership, it's best that you drop your "nice-guy" persona. So, if you ever assume the role of a parent, a coach, a teacher, a boss—it's best to drop the "nice-guy" persona and muster up the courage to be difficult.

Take a look at a few examples:

Example #1: Boss situation: You have been promoted to a new sales rep position and asked to drastically improve sales for a company. You lead a team of fifty sales agents.

If you adopt a "nice-guy" persona, you will allow the sales team a lot of autonomy; you will treat them as your equal; you will make sure no one's feelings are hurt; you will accommodate their needs; you will grow to care about them. What happens? The sales team loves you . . . but, because the sales team doesn't fear you, they will most certainly underperform. (Oh, I know there is a counterpoint here that says that because the sales team loves you soooooooooo much that they will actually overachieve for you. Bullshit. More likely that they will take advantage of your "nice-guy" persona and ultimately underperform.) This will lead to your failure and may cost people on the sales team to be terminated.

Now assume you drop the "nice-guy" persona. You will let it be known that you are in charge; you will demand accountability; you won't care about being liked; you won't make things easy; you won't be looking for friendship. What happens? The sales team won't love you. But they will respect you or, at least, they will respect your position as their leader. They will fear you. They will produce for you. This will lead to your success and will ultimately benefit the sales team by way of bigger paychecks, bigger bonuses, and better job security. So, you see, the people on the sales team will come to realize that they didn't need a friend. They needed a boss!!!!!!!!!!

Example #2: Parents: You just brought a few children into the world, and you now have the tremendous task of raising them to reach their full potential and to become fine citizens. The "nice guy" in us will allow them a lot of freedom, will want to make things easy for them, will care about their standing in various social circles, will allow rules to be bent and broken for fear of making them angry at us, will want to be their friend. What happens? The kids really, really, really like you (how comforting). They see themselves as being on equal footing with you. They don't fear you. They take advantage of your generosity; they become accustomed to being rescued; they do not reach their full potential. Later in life, they blame you (rightfully so) for not being tougher on them.

Now assume you drop the "nice-guy" persona. You make it clear that there is a hierarchy; you set rules and stick to them without exception; you make it clear that your motive and objective is not to be their friend; you don't always make things easy for them; you're indifferent to their social circumstances; your approval rating with them is near zero. What happens? The kids won't like you, but they will respect you or, at least, they will respect your position as being their parent. They will fear you. They will learn to get out of difficult situations on their own. They reach their full potential. Later in life they will thank you for having the courage to make things difficult. So, you see, the kids will later come to realize that they didn't need a friend. They needed a parent!!!!!!!!!!!

I'll say it again:

- *If you're going to assume the role of a leader, lose the "nice-guy" mentality.*
- *You don't always have to be a "nice guy."*

- *There are times when you have to force yourself to be a bitch or a prick.*
- *People will later appreciate you for not being so nice in instances when they needed more than a friend.*

If you cannot muster up the courage to drop the "nice-guy" persona, then don't assume roles that require leadership.

ANXIETY/DEPRESSION

So:

- There is a big test in the morning, and you didn't really study hard enough for it.
- You just found out that a loved one was involved in an accident, but you haven't been given many of the details.
- You got caught doing something that you shouldn't have been doing, and the consequences are uncertain.
- Your kid just got his license and is driving late at night by himself.
- You've taken on a bigger workload than you can handle, and it seems like everything is due all at the same time.

Naturally, you start to get nervous and anxious and you start to have all the unsettling emotions associated therewith, like restlessness and shakiness, and your brain goes into a bit of a panic mode. For the record, this is not problematic anxiety that warrants treatment. These are very natural emotions to real-life events that are actually happening. Life will present some very unfortunate situations and events, and we will all have to go through periods in our life that warrant feelings of nervousness and anxiety. And when this happens, we are just going to have to deal with it, get through it, and try to find ways to prevent those situations or events from happening again.

Problematic anxiety is when your brain is releasing those same feelings of nervousness, anxiety, and shakiness when there is no real-life event that is actually taking place. There is no big test in the morning; nobody has been involved in an accident; you didn't get busted; your kid is only six-years-old and won't be driving for another ten years. But your brain is playing the "what-if" game and it can be brutal:

- What if I run someone over on my way to work?
- What if I can't find a job?
- What if I go broke?
- What if a loved one dies?

Your brain is creating situations that warrant feelings of nervousness and anxiety, *but those situations are not really happening* and sometimes have no basis in reality. Oh yeah, and just to make it even more fun, your brain repeats the same thoughts over and over again. This is problematic anxiety.

Depression is kind of the same in that it involves the prolonged, constant, and continuous thoughts of doom, gloom, and sadness.

And just like with anxiety, there are going to be moments in life that warrant feelings of sadness. Depression, though, will cause you to have continuous and constant feelings of sadness even when there are no real-life events that warrant those feelings. Sometimes a change in the season is enough to bring on the blues. So, you see, nobody has died; no one is sick; you have a good job; you have a great family—but your brain is releasing feelings of doom, gloom, and sadness.

Your brain plays out worst-case scenarios over and over and over, and it is exhausting to the point that it interferes with all of the other things you could be and should be accomplishing. It's like a broken record that continues to repeat the same verse over and over again, and the verse is a negative thought (What if we go broke, what if we go broke . . . what if we go broke?).

Depression is just that: it robs you of your ability to keep things in proper perspective and robs you of being able to enjoy life.

So, what are the life lessons? What if you or a loved one suffers from problematic anxiety and/or depression? Here are my random thoughts:

- Yes, there are medicines and, yes, they work and, yes, you should take the meds. I've heard other people say that they don't want themselves or their kid to be on Prozac. Yet, when they or their kids have a cold or a fever then medicine is okay? So, medicine for physical ailments is okay for these people, but no meds for mental ailments????? It's a stigma.

- Therapy is a yes. I haven't done it (yet), but I believe the more help you can get, the better.

- Do talk to others about it, as you'll be surprised by the great many people who suffer, and maybe they have some advice for dealing and coping.

- Music is huge. Before you go to bed at night, play a song that makes you feel good and just repeat the lyrics. It's awesome when you wake up and your brain is singing the song instead of repeating the bad thoughts.

- Open your eyes. Yes, this is a simple one for temporary relief. When you're depressed, it feels like your brain is compressed and you tend to squint. Open your eyes and lift those eyebrows way up high and feel the compression lifted.

- Confront and even play out the bad situation as if it's happening. In other words, instead of running away from the negative thoughts, actually act like they are happening in real life or role-play it out. Maybe you'll come to learn that the fear of something is much greater than the thing itself.

- You just have to remind yourself of other times in your life when you have gone through these same feelings and came out of it. *Muscle through it.*

- A true panic attack is when the constant and continuous feelings are so strong that you actually pass out. Very scary.

- Stay focused on the immediate task at hand, however small it may be—"I'm making breakfast"; "I'm getting dressed"—don't let your mind wander off.

- Make a written list of positive things that are actually happening in your life, things that you should be grateful for, and some of your accomplishments. Read the list at various parts of the day.

- Another strategy is to compartmentalize. In other words, don't try to dismiss the negative thoughts altogether. Instead, tell yourself that you will deal with those thoughts at a certain time of the day, but not now. This part of the day is reserved for a different specific task; other parts of the day are reserved for other tasks, and then at a certain other part you will allow yourself to deal with the negative thoughts.

WHEN YOU'RE WRONG OR MAKE A MISTAKE

You just did something that you shouldn't have done or made a mistake and got busted. We are human, so there are bound to be many blunders on a daily basis, such as:

- Motor vehicle violation
- Cheating at school
- Ate all the cookies without leaving a single one for others
- Went to bed without checking the doors, only to realize that the family slept with the front door open
- You're the one who didn't flush that beauty of a turd.
- You're late.
- You forgot.

And now you are being confronted with the situation. You have two options:

Option #1: deny/deny/deny: That's right, shift the burden onto someone else, or place the blame on some fortuitous event over which you had no control. After all, your reputation is at stake and who wants to be known as a cheater, rule breaker, pig, or idiot. This will certainly place the situation in some doubt. There will be a lot of drama, as everyone has to dig in to defend themselves and others will be asked to choose sides. The problem here is that if someone has come to the point of confronting you with the situation, there is also a good chance that they already know what you know. That's right. They already know that it was you and/or it was your fault. So now, not only will you be known as the cheat, the pig, the rule breaker or the idiot, but on top of that you have imputed probably the worst character trait anyone can possibly possess—*lying*. This will take a while to sort through, will involve others, will lead to all kinds of resentment. I wouldn't be surprised if the percentage of people who react with option #1 is way, way up there. But there is a second option.

Option #2: admit/learn/never let it happen again: This sounds easy, but as humans I think our instincts always gravitate us toward option #1. Maybe it's because we are caught off guard or maybe we don't want to suffer the humiliation. We actually have to be aware that there is a second option, and we have to reprogram ourselves. Now when you are confronted, the person who is accusing you is fully expecting your reaction to be that of option #1 and the entire shit show and drama that comes with it. But, instead, with option #2 your reply will immediately diffuse the situation—"You're right, it was my fault. I am sorry. I'm really not going to try and make any excuse for it other than to say that I hope it didn't cause any serious problem. I will do my best to make sure it doesn't happen again." End of story. No one else was brought into it. Drama over. The person who brought this up may actually be disappointed. You see, now you are known to possess probably the best character trait a human can have—someone who tells the truth, even at the expense of some humiliation. Funny thing is you probably won't even impute the entire negative character trait that brought this up. Instead of being labeled a cheat, pig, or idiot, you'll be remembered for having that one-time lapse but otherwise *solid*. Like I said, easier said than done, but once you learn to pull it off, you solidify yourself as a much better friend, family member, employee/ employer, and person.

WHEN YOU'RE RIGHT

I was taught that when you are wrong, admit that what you did is wrong, take your punishment, and take steps to ensure that it doesn't happen again. This is good wisdom.

On the flip side, I was taught, "when you're right, *fight*." And with that ideology comes: when you're right, stand up for yourself. Don't be a doormat. Hold your ground. Don't let others take advantage of you. Defend your position and see it to the end. In retrospect, I don't think this is the best wisdom.

I think the following is better: know when to choose your battles.

I have come to learn that if you pick every battle in which you are right, you will become a miserable fuck and you can potentially go broke (emotionally and possibly financially). There will be many, many times when you are right, but the smart thing for you to do is *not* to fight. Not to defend your position. Not to argue. Swallow some pride and move along. But do so knowing that you have not wasted a lot of emotional energy nor financial resources trying to prove a point.

I have seen people spend fortunes defending themselves on a matter of "principle," only to later realize it wasn't worth it—financially or emotionally.

So, the new wisdom on "when you are right": weigh the pros and cons of the fight to prove you're right, then decide if the fight is worth it. In other words, choose your battles.

BECOME "OUTCOME-ORIENTED" (HAVE THE END IN MIND)

So:

- You are in a dispute with a loved one or a friend.
- You are about to enter a big meeting.
- You are about to confront someone.
- You are going into an interview.
- You are on a sales call.

When you are in these types of situations, the idea is to always have the end in mind.

Think and ask yourself, "how do I want to this to end?"

That will steer the discussion toward your wanted outcome. If you don't have the end in mind, many times the discussion/dispute will just go in its own direction and the outcome is uncertain. And then, it doesn't end the way you wanted.

If you had only put in the time in the beginning to formulate how you wanted it to end, then maybe the outcome would be different. This is particularly true when you're in a fight/dispute with someone.

Figure out the solution first, then engage. At least this way you are working toward the solution as opposed to just spewing out unwanted feelings and emotions.

PEOPLE OF AUTHORITY (RESPECT)

Doctors, teachers, coaches, priests, parents, elderly, police.

Old wisdom: The above people of authority are to be treated with respect. By virtue of the status that they have achieved, they are entitled to our respect and trust. Their position has earned them the right to be free from our scrutiny.

Well, maybe there was a time for that way of thinking, but it is kind of ludicrous. These are the people who we are entrusting with our health, our children, our overall well-being. I think that way too many of us were brainwashed into believing that these people of authority deserved a free pass simply by virtue of their status.

I believe that our "free pass" mentality allowed these people of authority to take advantage of their status and commit some of the most heinous crimes imaginable.

If you haven't done so already, you will encounter countless stories of the doctor who prescribed the wrong treatment, the coach who allowed the hazing, the priest who stole the money, the parent who abused the kids, etc.

It is the *old wisdom* that allowed the great majority of these travesties to take place.

New wisdom: Treat people of authority like all others. They need to earn our respect. As a matter of fact, we should actually scrutinize these people even more than the common person, as we are entrusting them with our livelihood and that of our families.

By no means am I advocating that we disrespect these people. What I am saying is that not only is it okay for us to challenge these people, but that we have a duty to do so. The great majority of these "people of authority" are solid, and those are the ones who will have no problems if they are challenged. It's those who feel that they somehow deserve a free pass that worry me. No one deserves a free pass. Each and every one of us must earn the respect of others, regardless of our status.

- To the doctor who failed to fully explain his diagnosis and treatment plan: it is your duty to demand from the doctor a full explanation and, further, that you fully expect him/her to treat you with compassion and respect.
- To the teacher who wants to overburden your kid with homework and projects: remind the teacher that both you and your kid have more going on in

your life than third grade social studies, and that perhaps they should also find other interests.

- To the coach who continues to run practice past the six-thirty end time: remind them that they are now on your time and suggest that they run a more efficient practice.
- To the priest who organizes an unsupervised retreat: It is our duty to scrutinize this arrangement. Yes, we share in the blame. The *old wisdom* of allowing the kids alone with the priest solely on account of the priest's status as a religious figure didn't work out so well. We share the blame.
- To the parent who continues to inflict feelings of guilt and emotional pain well into adulthood: no more—your status as a parent confers no right to such monstrous behavior.
- To the cop who exceeds his authority: remind him/ her that there is a chain of command, and that he/ she is not at the top.

It's funny how we have all been trained into somehow being afraid to confront these people, and that has just allowed them to perpetuate their inconsiderate and/or criminal behaviors. No more free passes!!!!!

FOCUS ON THE GOOD

Look, things are never going to be 100% perfect. But, if you have worked hard, if you have prepared, if you have put thought into things, and if you are lucky, most often things may be 70% perfect, even 80%–90% sometimes, and on some occasions getting damn near 100% perfect. Unfortunately, we rarely achieve that 100% perfection and it's amazing how we allow ourselves to focus on the small percentage in a given situation that isn't going quite right. This is true of almost everything that is happening. A few examples:

Example #1: You are at a great restaurant; you are with a fun group of people, having great conversations—but they put you at a table near the door.

Example #2: Your job is rewarding; you are made to feel appreciated, good money, good boss—but it would be so much better if it were closer to home.

Example #3: A friend of yours (Debbie) has helped you out before; she is dependable, sympathetic, and trustworthy—but she won't let you get a word in.

The list of examples goes on and on. Situations are not perfect, and people are not perfect. But why in the world would we ever allow ourselves to focus on the small part of the situation or person who is no good when the majority and, sometimes, the great majority of what is happening is great.

The lesson is to to focus on the large percentage of good things that are happening in a situation or with a person. It's your choice as to what you will focus on. Will you focus on the small percentage that isn't going quite right and become a nag, a complainer, a miserable fuck? Fuck that. Choose to focus on the high percentage of things in a situation that are going great. The best way to do this is to talk up the great things that are happening in a situation, and soon enough the negative stuff gets drowned out in your sea of positivity. Talk up the good stuff. Go ahead, repeat it. Talk it up, man. Live in the good stuff. Let others live in the small percentage. And, if you get really good at it, you'll find a way to turn the small negatives into positives.

#1: Man, this restaurant is great and I am so happy to be with this crowd. I'm actually glad we got this table because our food seems to be coming out faster.

#2: I am so glad that I have a job, a job that I like, a job that is rewarding. With my long commute, I am going to listen to some music I haven't heard in a while.

#3: Debbie is great. She has helped me out in times of need; we have similar interests and perspectives. I am going to let her know how I appreciate all of her positive qualities. Thank goodness she is in a talkative mood because who really feels like talking.

Focus on the positive. Talk up the positives. Drown out the negatives.

What about when it's 90% bad? The same technique applies, in the sense that you have to find a way to focus on the 10% that's good and remind yourself that it is temporary. If you ever master this skill, you will probably have to keep it quiet. You see, when things are 90% bad and you have somehow found a way to get through situations focusing in on the small percentage that is good, people will judge you to be an unsympathetic, cold-hearted prick. I don't know. I just find it to be a strategic coping mechanism, but maybe psychologists will tell you that you have to allow yourself to live in that 90% miserable existence when it is happening. It's unfortunate that others who have chosen to focus on the negative feel that all others must also choose to live in that same miserable existence. They just don't realize that we have made a conscious choice to focus on the small percentage of the situation that is positive, as a way of getting through the same exact situation that they are going through. Not sure why they think they have the right to judge us. We are both going through the same situation. They have chosen to be miserable and to stay miserable. We are trying to get past it.

MARRIAGE

This one is kind of easy.

Put your spouse ahead of everyone else in your life (including yourself) and you will have a solid marriage.

In life, we have to deal with friends, family, and our spouse. We owe a certain degree of commitment and loyalty to each. Naturally, we want to try to please everyone and most of the time we can.

Problems arise when we have to please one person at the expense of another. Your mom or dad wants it done a certain way, but your spouse wants it done their way. Easy. Tell your parents to take a back seat; remind them that your spouse provides you with the love and support to get you through every minute of every day, and for that reason you owe your spouse a higher level of commitment and loyalty that you owe them. Yes, it will sting and yes, you will feel bad, but your family and friends need to know where you stand. *Spouse first*—they are somewhere farther down.

Do this as early in a marriage as possible so that all the riffraff know where you stand, and there will be so much less drama in your life. If your friends or family think that they are on equal footing with your spouse, then you are in for a lot of drama, as they will put you in positions that will make you miserable. Shame on them for thinking that they are on equal footing with your spouse, and shame on them for putting you in tough positions. But shame more on you for not having put them in their place a long time ago.

You can be as delicate as you want in letting family and friends know where they stand, but I think its best to proclaim it *boldly* and *loudly. My spouse comes first and you need to fuck off.* If you and your spouse jointly do this, you're in for a happy marriage.

Oh yeah, another thing, don't ever belittle whatever your spouse is saying or doing. That's another big one.

WANTS/NEEDS

Life can be made very simple if you can successfully define a particular desire as a "want" or a "need." That is, we should ask ourselves, "is what I desire something that I need, or is it merely something that I want?"

The easy rule is that if something is "needed," go out and get it. If there is no need for a particular item, let it go.

That which is needed will be cherished and maintained.

That which is "wanted" will not be used to its full potential; it will be soon be unappreciated or underappreciated; it will be neglected; and it will be discarded.

When we merely fulfill something that we "want," it is a temporary fix. Soon, we will move on to something else that we want, and so on, and so on. Given that it does not fulfill any real "need," it will not be appreciated.

For example, a young adult can make a very strong argument for the "need" of a vehicle. Indeed, a vehicle can allow the young adult to become more self-sufficient and independent, obtain employment, and assist with other family chores. So, allow them to make their case and allow them to phrase the question . . . and, "therefore, I need a vehicle," instead of . . . "and, therefore, I want a Jeep."

Look, we are all super spoiled. It is very difficult sometimes to deprive ourselves of what we want. We are constantly being bombarded with the "latest and greatest." We have allowed ourselves to be surrounded by people who fulfill each and every want that their heart desires.

Be the smart one. Allow others to show off. They will soon realize the stupidity of their purchases, and they will soon become very envious of your ability to show restraint.

They key is to have the dough ($) for when a "need" arises. It will be a stress-free event. Because I haven't wasted all my money on unnecessary "wants," I have the dough right here and right now for this need—Done! Easy!

Those who have blown their money on needless items will be forced to scramble when a true "need" arises.

Kind of strange. Look around you. Those who live to fulfill their needs are living relatively stress-free. Those who seem to have everything under the sun, seem to be very stressed and financially burdened.

So, just ask: Is this something that I need? Or is it something that I want?

IS TODAY THE DAY?

I'm not really sure that I should devote a whole chapter to this, but I learned this lesson only recently and I think it can have a very positive impact on how we live our lives.

Nobody likes to think about death all that much. Rightfully so. But death is kind of a random thing. Most of us take living and being alive for granted.

Try this and see if you can handle it.

When you get up in the morning, ask yourself "Is today the day? Is it my number?"

Wow! Kind of scary, isn't it!!!!!! The thought that any day can be the day.

If today is your day, then it will have a huge impact on how you live that day!!!!!!! Suddenly, everything is put in its proper perspective. What we think are "important events" or "important decisions" that need to be made are suddenly extremely trivial.

The results of the test, the final episode of the TV series that is airing at 7:00 p.m., the phone conversation you have planned with your friend to gossip, the results you are expecting at work, the outcome of a project you have been working on—I think you get it. If you start your day asking "is today the day?" all of this will be put into its proper perspective.

Most likely, we will gravitate toward what is important to us. Our family, our friends, our loved ones. We will probably make the effort to reach out to these people, spend time with these people, tell these people how much we love them.

Make this part of your morning routine. As you're brushing your teeth, go ahead and ask the question . . . Is today the day? It will serve as a reminder that every day should be considered special. We should enter every day with a certain amount of perspective. If today is the day, boy, oh boy, will that make certain decisions easy to make.

BE HUMBLE

- You got into your dream school.

- You rocked the midterm.

- You own lots of property.

- You got a raise.

- You have a lot of money in savings.

- You got asked out by that special someone.

- You look good.

- You're making a lot of money.

- Your kid made the "A" team.

The lesson here is real simple: Keep it to yourself. Be humble.

There is absolutely no need to for you to tell *anyone* any of the above info. Yep, that includes great friends and relatives. Most people are jealous. We are wired that way. If you dare tell anyone any of the above, that will have an effect on your relationship with them—and it will not be a positive effect. Most people will not be happy for you. Oh, they may say how happy they are for you but, instead, their jealousy will kick in; or worse, they will use the above against you. Once you blurt it out, people will tell you how great it is for you; but most people will secretly resent you for having advanced, and here is what they are probably thinking:

- You got into your dream school: you got in only because you took all of those prep classes costing megabucks, and because your family has connections.

- You rocked the midterm: that's because the professor likes you.

- You own other property: you must have other sources of income or maybe you come from a wealthy family.

- You got a raise: you're a brownnoser.

- You have a lot of money in savings: it's because you are so cheap.

- You got asked out by that special someone: you must be "easy."

- You look good: it's probably all fake.

- You're making a lot of money: well, maybe you should start picking up more tabs.

- Your kid made the "A" team: it's because the coach likes you, and because of all that money you spent on trainers.

I'll say it again. Whatever positives you have going on in your life, *be humble. Keep it to yourself.* Look, people will most likely come to "learn" or "suspect" all of the above about you. But, if you haven't come out and said it, then there is some doubt and people will not be as jealous or resentful.

The goal is for you to try to always create an appearance as being on equal footing with others. It is a lot easier to maintain friendships and relationships when you are on equal footing and not constantly trying to "one-up" each other.

I have had the opportunity to meet and be friends with both kinds of people. Some are glad to let me know everything they have accumulated, what they are making, etc. The problem is that I am not impressed by all that crap, so it does absolutely nothing to impress me. Another friend is the opposite. Oh, I know he has it made. Not because he told me, but because of other things that I can pick up on. Never, ever, has he tried to impress me. Instead, he has always made sure that whatever we do, that he tones it down to my level. Then, when there is that once-in-a-lifetime occasion where he knows it's out of my financial league (think Super Bowl), he sets a price that he knows I can afford and makes it seem like he got a great deal. Guess who I am more impressed with?????

Similarly, don't seek out any of the above information from others. It's none of your business.

Typically, the person who shows off the most, has the least. The person who you can't get a read on because he/she isn't very revealing, has the most. They just don't want you to know, for fear that it may ruin your relationship.

There is a famous saying: *"Speak softly and carry a big stick."* My take on it is to not let people know too much about you ("speak softly"), but when they independently find shit out about you, make sure that what they find out is greater than they would have imagined ("carry a big stick"). *Bam*!!!!!!!!

So, you see, don't tell people how you are getting all As in your classes. If asked, give a generic response: "I'm doing pretty well." Keep them in suspense. If they ever take their investigation to the next level and independently find out that you're a straight A student . . . now, not only are they impressed with your academic achievement, but they also appreciate you for your humility.

SAY "YES" (GET OUT OF YOUR COMFORT ZONE)

"No." "Nope." "Sorry, I can't." "Nah." "Not interested." Sound familiar?

Try and think about some of the things that you may have said "no" to recently:

- A client asks you to go out for lunch.
- The family asks to try a new restaurant.
- You got asked to go watch the game.
- Friends want to go on a trip.
- Try a new route to get to the same place.
- Receive an invite from someone who isn't really a friend
- Go see an attraction that you live near.
- Friends ask you to go out.
- Try a new workout routine.

I get it. There are times that we have to say "no" because we have a conflict or perhaps it's not in the budget.

But many times we say "no" simply out of convenience and an unwillingness to get out of our "comfort zones." I suppose we all create our own identities and comfort zones and proceed to live within those parameters. Then, when we are confronted with something new or something that requires a bit of effort, we default to "no." *Lame.*

Why do we say "no"? Why are we unwilling to get out of our comfort zone? A big part of it is laziness. That is something you have to change. Life is too short to sit in front of the TV, especially when there are more meaningful alternatives. Get off the fucking couch.

The other part is a fear of failure. That's right, we don't do things because we fear that they will be deemed failures (having a bad experience). But you have to stop and think about it and put things in perspective. These are not life-and-death decisions.

Some of the best memories in life come out of moments and events that are complete failures. Think: Indiana Dunes (Gary, Indiana). Come on, it wasn't that bad. But we won't be going back anytime soon—that's for sure. It becomes more about who you are with than what you are doing.

Is it better to try something new and have "bad" experiences with others, as opposed to staying home and having a "safe" experience alone????

BEING INDIFFERENT

I have met many people who are very opinionated on a vast array of topics. Indeed, I think that the great majority of all people hold strong opinions on all the big and not-so-big issues. We have some big, divisive issues that sort of welcome a strong opinion from each of us. A few of the biggies include:

- Republican vs. Democrat

- Capital punishment

- Abortion

- Best way to stimulate the economy

- How best to raise kids

It seems that I have spent my entire lifetime listening to my family, close friends, and casual acquaintances boldly and passionately take a stand on these issues. Some will then go on to articulate the reasons in support of their position and, within this group, some are much better than others at being able to support their position. What's happening when people set forth their position is usually twofold.

First, the part that boldly sets forth a person's position *is based upon emotion and passion*: "I am very much in support of capital punishment, and we shouldn't be afraid to use it more often than we already do."

Then, the part that articulates the supporting reasons *is based upon intellect*: "By having capital punishment in place for not only capital crimes but for even lesser offenses, people will be deterred from committing the crimes in the first place." I believe that intellect is both an innate quality and something that can be gained through education and learning.

You have the emotion/passion that's driving the core position, and then you have the intellect that is used to support the position.

I have always hated people who boldly and passionately set forth their position ("Fry them criminal bastards."), but then lack the intellect to articulate any intelligent supporting reasons. This, of course, can be a character flaw on my part because some people just don't have the mental capacity to adequately articulate supporting reasons (well, then maybe they should shut up and listen to people who do have it—sorry, but it's a serious character flaw). I like to quickly end discussions with these people and just as quickly create some distance. "You're right, fry them for an extra long time. I have to go to the bathroom now." See ya!!!!!!!

Then you have the people who boldly and passionately set forth their position and proceed to articulate one or several supporting reasons. I have always hated these people as well. Maybe more. You see, these people possess the intellect to know not only the supporting reasons for their core belief, but they also possess the intellect to know that the rationales are flawed (studies have shown that in states with capital punishment, crime rates remain unchanged or have gone up), have holes in them (innocent people have been put to death), and are subject to scrutiny (lethal injection may not lead to a fast and instantaneous death as originally thought). Yet, these people are able to still somehow boldly and passionately manifest their belief about something and to somehow set aside their intelligence. This has often caused me to go back and try and find the last guy I was talking to—you know, the guy who lacked the intellect—where did he go????

I have always felt that you should know both sides of every argument, and that you should be able to articulate reasons both in support and against whatever it is that is being discussed. Look, every meaningful topic has pros and cons. There is no argument that is not without fault and flaws.

The problem is when you think this way, you become *indifferent*. That is, you don't take a firm stand on anything. When you see the pros and cons in everything, you fail to take a strong position on anything and by allowing yourself to become indifferent, you begin to lack emotion and passion.

Those of us who have become indifferent have allowed our intellect to take away our passion and emotion. This is wrong. There needs to be a better balance between the emotion/passion and the intellect. Being indifferent is just as bad as the moron who boldly and passionately sets forth a position but is then unable to articulate any reasons in support of such position. By being indifferent, you allow yourself to engage in an endless intellectual tennis match with a never-ending volley of back-and-forth positions—no conclusion, no winner. End it already. Take a stand. Sure, your position is flawed, it has holes in it, and it is subject to scrutiny. *But, too bad, it's better to be a passionate fool than a lethargic, intellectual waste.*

I am done being on the sidelines. I am now entering the playing field with all of you other idiots who have allowed yourself to put aside some of your smarts. I just wish that someone had told be before that it is sometimes okay to put aside some of the smarts and join in on the fun. I'm going out and getting some boxing gloves. Here we go!!!!!!!

Capital punishment—that's letting people off too easy. How's that for starters?

MONEY

There is that one famous saying: "Money cannot buy you happiness." I'm not sure who originally said it. It is now used by people on both sides of the money debate. You know, those with a lot of dough will claim that they were happy to begin with, and that the money has little to do with their current state of happiness. How convenient. Then you have those who don't have any dough, and they will claim that you can be broke, hungry, cold, and happy all at the same time. Really????

Well I didn't grow up poor, so I can't give any firsthand accounts as to the ability to find happiness at a time where you are struggling for survival. I won't even go there with this discussion other than to say that for the truly poor, I have to imagine that money can provide happiness in the form of food, clothing, and shelter. So, for the truly poor, let's end the debate—money can buy happiness.

But what about for the next level? Those people who cannot be classified as "poor" but who don't have a big stash of money. This group has to work very hard for their money, and they don't have a trust fund to rescue them in times of need. Can money buy these people happiness? Yes, of course it can. I'm not sure that is the right question. Look, money can buy happiness, so let's rephrase the question.

How about this: Are there any benefits to those who are struggling financially or moments in life when you are struggling financially?

I'll say it again. I was never poor, and the only times that I can ever be classified as "struggling" financially is when I tried to break my financial dependence from my hardworking parents. Two occasions come to mind: The first is when I went off to law school, and the second is right after I got married. In each occasion, it was a matter of pride to break my dependence from the gravy train. When I went away to law school, I knew that my parents were already footing the big-ticket tab of tuition and housing, so I didn't want to hit them up for money on books, the cost of a computer, and spending money. Then, when I first got married, well this was my first real test of financial independence, and I didn't want to blow it. In each occasion, I wasn't truly "poor" as I had a safety net, but I was determined not to use it. So, there I was at moments in my life with less money than I was accustomed to. Was I happy??? Well, I can certainly remember a lot of good times, so I am not going to say that I was miserable by any stretch of the imagination. I think I can appreciate those times for having taught me—

- How to be frugal and proud of it: No better feeling than paying a lot less for something than everyone else. Love it.
- How to save: It's a great feeling to watch that savings account grow. If you want to break free of your dependence, have the money saved up.
- Have a stronger work ethic: I was looking to make more money, and it's kind of an easy formula— more work = more money.

So, I'll ask again, during these times that I was "struggling financially," was I happy??? You bet. Are you kidding me??? I went from being dependent on others to standing on my own two feet. Struggling financially is what gave me my drive. In law school, it was probably more like baby steps by not constantly asking for money. It was a good feeling to say "no thanks" when my parents asked if I needed some money. Then when I first got married, I was driven to make it on my own. To do so, I was going to have to work very hard, learn to be frugal, and save my money. I can honestly say that I am very grateful for those times in my life when I had the least money. *Some of my strongest character traits are directly attributable to those moments in my life when I was struggling financially.*

So, are there any benefits to those who are struggling financially? Absolutely. Many positive character traits are formed, and those with less truly appreciate things more.

So, what about those who have made it? Those who we consider rich? They have worked hard, they have saved wisely, and they have a grip on their big-ticket bills. Can money buy them happiness??? You bet ya. It's great to have a wad of cash, take vacations, splurge on a good meal, buy that outfit that makes you look good. I think that this is particularly true for those people who have worked hard for their money. This is their reward. They are entitled to it. They deserve it. So yes, happiness can be derived from having an abundance of money.

However, there is a point of diminishing returns. There is a point for the wealthy where extra money does not equate to extra happiness. There is most definitely a threshold. After the third vacation this year, is the fourth going to be all that special, or will it be looked at as interfering with a normal schedule???? After eating out at all the fancy steak houses four straight nights this week, is our upcoming dinner at Ruth's Chris going to be all that special? I think you get it. The extra money is not buying you extra happiness and is probably doing you harm.

So, the life lesson is clear. It's not always a good thing to have an abundance of money. It can actually be a good thing to struggle. This can create a strong work ethic. It can teach you to be frugal and save. It can help you to appreciate what you have. Lots of good things come out of a struggle.

YOU'RE REALLY NOT
THAT IMPORTANT

We all have various roles in life. Many of us are spouses, parents, employees, employers, etc. There will be a point in your life (and hopefully many) when you become very good at what you do within that certain role. It's a great feeling. There are many, many positives:

- You are efficient.
- You can multitask.
- You can do more.
- You are in charge.
- Others rely on you.

But there will also be some negatives:

- You take on more.
- You become cocky.
- Others rely too much on you.
- You don't delegate.

And then, you begin to see yourself and/or your role as "vital" or "crucial" or "pivotal," and you start to think that you are more important than you really are. The consequence? You begin to forgo other opportunities; you devote far too much time to your one role; you refuse to do fun things; you miss out on family and friend get togethers; you don't exercise; you put aside more meaningful things in life. Why? Because you feel that the work won't get done; the task will not get accomplished; the project won't get finished; others can't possibly handle situations without you.

I'm here to tell you that you are really not that important. You can be replaced. The work will get done; the project will get finished; the task will get accomplished; others are capable of handling situations without you. Realize that someone else is capable of doing what you do, maybe not as efficiently or as professionally, but more than good enough.

The lesson, of course, is not to forgo the more meaningful aspects of life (family vacations, family dinners, your health) on account of your ego. That's right, it's an ego problem. You have come to see yourself as much more important than you really are. Are you here on this planet solely to show off your work skills????? Life will go on without you at the helm. It will. So break away. Allow someone else to pick up the slack.

I feel bad when I hear someone say that they haven't gone on a vacation in five years, that they missed some family event, that they can't possibly go at that time of year—all because they feel that they are more important than they really are. Shit will get done, with or without you.

You always hear of people's regrets from having devoted far too much time to their job, profession, craft, or whatever. And then, when it's all over, they wished that they had devoted more time to their family. Don't ever allow yourself to become that person.

The world will find a way to move on without you. You actually aren't all that important in the larger scope of things, so don't ever think that what you do is so critical that your failure to do it will somehow lead the world to stop. It won't.

DON'T CHASE THE
WRONG THINGS

If you look at our culture today, you see that our society wants us to strive for wealth, materialistic items, status, higher positions. Fuck that.

If you chase that stuff, you will end up feeling empty, as your triumphs will be short-lived and lonely. In order to achieve what society is selling, you will have to sell out on what is truly important. Instead of chasing the wrong things, start chasing more meaningful things and remember:

"The way to get meaning into your life is to devote yourself to loving others, devote yourself to your community around you, and devote yourself to creating something that gives you purpose and meaning."

—Morrie Schwartz, *Tuesdays with Morrie*

This may be the highlight of the entire book, so I hope you have read this far along. If you haven't done so already, get off of the fucking crazy train to Emptyville and Lonelyville, and call a loved one or a friend; go do some volunteer work; devote yourself to a higher cause. Don't chase the next house, the next car, the next job. What you have right now is probably plenty.

LOYALTY

Loyalty is certainly a very important character trait. It's the quality of being faithful to someone or something.

I used to think that loyalty was way up there in terms of positive quality traits, but I have come off of that position lately.

I still understand the importance of loyalty. You want people to know that you appreciate them, you have their back, and they can count on you to back them up. So:

- You have been chosen to be a captain and you are picking teams. You have a friend who isn't as good as others. Out of loyalty to your friend, you pick him even though you know he sucks.
- Your employer has put a lot of time, money, and effort into training you for your current position. A competitor makes you a job offer with slightly better terms. Out of loyalty to your employer, you stay put.

So yes, being loyal is still important and will most likely be rewarded.

But loyalty can get you into a whole lot of trouble.

You see, you might be confronted with situations where a family member, a friend, a boss, or a co-worker has done something wrong, and you are confronted with one of the following situations:

- Your spouse was driving drunk and hit someone and left the scene of the accident. The police have called you and are asking if you know anything about this.
- Your friend stole someone's wallet, and you know that has caused the victim many problems. The victim confronts you.
- Your boss is intentionally falsifying the company's financial documents in an effort to overvalue the company's stock price. Government regulators are asking if you know anything about this.
- Your co-worker is lying on his timesheets, which is costing the company money. Your boss has asked if you know of any irregularities.

So, you see how this loyalty thing isn't so easy. In each of the above instances, the great majority of us would protect our spouse, friend, boss, and co-worker primarily out of loyalty, and you can see in each instance how it is wrong.

Indeed, protecting them can and probably will also get you in trouble. So, as good of a quality trait as loyalty is, it can come at a significant cost.

So the lesson has to be:

- Be loyal to yourself first. You owe a higher duty of loyalty to yourself than you do to others. In situations where others have put you in a dilemma, you have to be selfish. If others have fucked up or are doing something wrong, put the burden back on them to make things right, and let them know not to put you in the position of having to do something you don't want to do.

You see, loyalty puts the burden on you to be faithful. But, if someone has done or is doing something wrong, you need to think about yourself, not them. Put the burden back on them.

Look up:

- Enron executives
- Joe Paterno/Jerry Sandusky/Penn State

The people involved paid dearly for being loyal.

If loyalty has put you in a spot where you are part of a "cover-up," you are doomed, as the cover-up is sometimes viewed as being just as bad as the original wrong.

I'm really not feeling the love anymore for this loyalty thing. I am even looking back at my two examples where loyalty is a good thing—you know, when you're the captain picking teams and then again when you receive a job offer from a competitor. I just don't know if loyalty is rewarded—and if it's not—then it needs to be further examined. A fine line for sure. But let's at least get away from the concept of being loyal to the point where it has the potential to bring you harm. Fuck that.

THE LAST TEN PERCENT

In life, we make various pledges to a certain religion, friend, boss, and even to ourselves, and with it comes responsibilities to do things that kind of suck.

- We are Catholic, so we attend Mass on Sunday mornings. Yes, we would rather sleep in, but attending Mass on Sunday mornings is a requirement, so get your ass in the pew and try and muscle through the next hour.
- We have friends, so we attend a function that they are hosting. It's an event that doesn't interest us much, is on a day and time that is inconvenient, and is being attended by others who we don't care for, but friendship dictates that we attend, so you can put me down as a "yes."
- We want to stay healthy, so we work out. It's a daily grind. But it's only forty-five minutes and it has its benefits, so let's not think about it and just get it done already.
- We have a job, so we work. The job dictates that we put in an eight-ten hour day, and 5:00 p.m. will come soon enough, so we show up.

Isn't life great? All right, I am being a bit sarcastic. But, I think you get it. We have responsibilities, and it's important that we keep our commitments—even when we wish we could be doing something else.

I've come to realize something about myself, but I really don't know the significance of it. Here is what I've come to recognize. I am a ten percenter. When it comes to the last ten percent, I have no problem bailing.

- When I attend Mass, I'll take communion and bail. After all, I don't really need to hear the priest tell me that the "Mass has ended and go in Peace," and then have to fight everyone getting out of church and the parking lot. The last 10% is grueling, and I'd prefer to skip it and beat the crowd.
- When I attend a function I don't want to be at, I'll make sure that the host has recognized my presence, and then I'll immediately start to come up with my exit strategy.
- As I'm working out, I always know how much I have completed and how much I have left to go. As I get closer to the end of the workout, I have no problem bailing on the last few sets. After all, I could hurt myself.
- It's Friday afternoon and its 4:45 p.m., everyone else at the office has left, and nobody would know if I stayed until 5:00 p.m. See ya.

As you can see, I am a ten percenter. Look, I take my responsibilities seriously and I am good about keeping my commitments. But, I have issues with the last 10%.

I never perceived this as a problem, and I still don't know if it warrants a chapter in this book. I've always sort of looked at it as outsmarting the situation. Sort of like the last 10% is for idiots, and it really isn't all that important. I've often looked at people who see things through the entire 100% and wondered, "what are they thinking?" or "why doesn't everyone think like I do and bail?"

There has to be some huge benefit to the last 10%, as the great majority of people see things through until the end.

I am struggling to learn the significance of the last 10%.

I can only suppose the significance of the last 10% is as follows:

- The last 10% is the toughest part so if you bail, you are not outsmarting people, you are quitting—*ouch*!!!!!
- The last 10% can start to become 20%, 30%, etc. and next thing you know, you have allowed yourself to become an unemployed, fat atheist with no friends.
- Others will recognize your ability to see things through till the end, no matter how difficult.

I am fairly certain that you have observed my approach on the last 10%, and that is what is bothering me. In my efforts to outsmart situations, have I inadvertently taught you that it is okay to bail???? Will this translate to more meaningful aspects in your life when you should stay the course and see things through until the end? This is bothersome.

It's kind of too late for me to preach to you the importance of the last 10%, but I sincerely hope I haven't made a mistake here. Please give this a lot more thought before you follow in my footsteps on this one.

Also, before you judge me too harshly on this, please recognize that I am also a ninety percenter. That is, I am very good about the first 90% of my commitments, and I hope you observed that part as well. Not just the last 10%. If that isn't good enough for you, you know.

IF YOU'RE NOT HAVING FUN—
THEN WHAT'S THE POINT?

I've come across a lot of famous quotes and sayings:

- "I exist and therefore I am."—Socrates
- "Do unto others as you would do unto yourself."—Bible
- "Life is without meaning; it's what meaning you bring to it that counts."—not sure
- "The reasonable man adapts himself to the world; the unreasonable man persists in trying to adapt the world to himself."—George Bernard Shaw

As you can see, these quotes come from some of the great philosophers, leaders, and books of all time. Many of the quotes have tremendous meaning and wisdom, and you can certainly use them as benchmarks to live a positive life. Yet, none of these famous quotes ever had that much of an effect on me. They never really made me stop and think twice about it. For all of their fame and notoriety, none of these famous sayings made me flat out stop and think about things.

There is one particular saying that I heard when I was in my late thirties that has had a lasting impact. It did flat out make me stop everything I was doing and everything I was thinking about. At that very moment that I read it, I knew it was a game changer for me. The funny thing is that the person who said it isn't some great scholar and really had no intention of saying anything profound. I guess you have to know the context in which it was said to appreciate its meaning and the impact it had on me.

Around 2007, we had a tremendous meltdown of our economy. They were talking about things getting as bad as the Great Depression. The stock market crashed; the real estate bubble burst; tons of jobs were lost—the writing was on the wall. It was constantly on the news, day after day, week after week, month after month, doom and gloom. This was going to affect all of us. Some more than others, but there was going to be an impact. And sure enough, there was.

Some of my clients lost everything. It was as if they were trying to keep a snow cone from melting in 100 degree weather. That snow cone was melting right in front of their eyes, and there wasn't anything that they or I could do to stop it. Then, a few close friends lost their jobs. That really hurt. It's difficult to see someone you know who has the responsibility as head of household have to go out and lower their head, swallow their pride, and ask for help with finding a job. The days turn into weeks, the weeks turn into months. You know it's a struggle for them. Next thing you know, you become a bit more distant with them, as every conversation inevitably leads to a discussion about the job loss and inability to find any meaningful substitute employment.

For some of us "lucky" ones, the impact involved making less money, worrying, cutting back on going out for dinner, worrying, revisiting our financial goals and aspirations, worrying, possibly not being able to go on the "annual guys' golf trip," oh yeah, and did I mention the constant worrying.

Then came the time of year when we usually put together the annual guys' golf trip. I was thinking that it would most likely be best if it just gets put on the back burner for a few years, just to allow everyone a chance to get back to some normalcy. It didn't seem right to splurge or even allow myself to get away in light of everything that was going on. But instead, it got thrown out there. Not sure who sent it out or the exact message, but it was kind of a generic, "Hey guys, maybe we should tone down the trip or put it off until next year."

Well, there was an immediate response from one of the guys who had gotten laid off. He explained that he could certainly not afford to go on a trip that we had been accustomed to, but he also explained that he thought that it was important for us to keep the annual trip alive at any level because, as he explained: *If you're not having fun, then what is the point?*

And there you have it. The quote that I have put ahead of the great Socrates and all those other geniuses. You see, yes:

- There is a time to worry.
- There is a time to be afraid.
- There is a time to cry.

But, you have to always, always be mindful that *if you're not having fun, what's the point*? So even in the worst of times, don't allow yourself to become a miserable fuck; don't allow what's happening around you to deprive yourself of the very core of our existence. If we are not having fun or planning something fun, then what's the point of being here? What's the point of living? To be miserable? To complain? To worry? To make others miserable? Fuck all that!!!!

I can't remember where we went on that particular golf trip. Who knows, maybe it was at one of those golf arcade games in one of the guys' basements, but I will always remember that in the face of all the worrying life will throw at us, we have to always, always, always have something fun on the horizon so that we have something to look forward to.

So the life lesson is to always have something fun on the horizon—whether it's a day, a week, or even a month from now so that you have something to look forward to and to get you through life's doom and gloom.

DOS/DON'TS/OTHER

- **DO hold the door open for the person coming in after you.** Even if you have to wait for them to pass through. If they don't acknowledge your kind gesture, feel free to tell them to fuck off.

- **DO go out of your way to say "thank you."** I'm not talking about the "at the moment" gesture of saying thanks. I am talking about "after the moment" gestures that can be as simple as an after-the-fact e-mail—"I just wanted to tell you how much fun I had" or "I just wanted to acknowledge how much I appreciated your help." Maybe even a small gift? You see, it's the "after-the-fact" gesture that will separate you from all others who said "thanks" and then quickly moved on.

- **DON'T talk badly about others.** There is a double whammy here. First, the person who you are talking badly about will most certainly find out, which will lead to unnecessary drama. Second, the people whom you are talking to will characterize you as someone who talks badly about others, and they will recognize that today you are talking badly about Suzie, and that tomorrow you are capable of talking badly about them. Similarly, when others start to talk badly about someone, rather than pile on, either stay silent or have something nice to say about the target like, "that all might be true, but Suzie was the only one who helped me." This will show others that you are capable of standing up for a friend.

- **DO give generous tips**. No one likes a cheap-ass. Normally the difference between leaving a 15% vs. a 20% tip is only a few bucks. A few bucks is not going to make or break you. If it only takes a few bucks to elevate you to being characterized as "generous," you may as well give the little bit extra. You'll feel better about it too.

- **DO interact with everyone**. Yep, the sanitation worker, the mail carrier, the person working the cash register, the cab driver, the janitor, the crossing guard, the parking attendant. A quick "sure is nice out today" can transform nonpersonable encounters we have with everyday people into something more. These people will recognize you as having treated them as your equal at that moment in time, regardless of each other's circumstances.

- **DON'T tailgate**. It's stupid. What's the point? To send a message? Really? You're just testing your reflexes, which is unnecessary.

- **DO work your ass off**. One of the best character traits you can posses is to work hard. Go the extra mile; put in the extra effort. Look, hard work may not immediately translate into success. However, there are other great benefits that come with working hard. At the end of the day, you will feel so much better about yourself knowing that you put in some extra time instead of catching up on Netflix shows and following up on social media. Others will also notice, and it's really a good thing to be characterized as a hard worker. Hard work will translate into success. Yes, there is a point where too much hard work can have negative consequences, but make sure you bring yourself to that crossroad many times in your life. The idea is to work your ass off at the expense of trivial things, such as watching TV and spending useless time on social media.

- **DON'T swear when you are among people who don't know you.** It really cheapens your brand. Save the F-bombs for when you are with your good friends, as they already know you for who you are.
- **DON'T interrupt people when they are talking**. That's right, listen and allow others to complete their thought. Then when it's your turn to talk, if they have the audacity to interrupt you, quickly interject, "Please allow me to finish my thought just as I did for you, you fucking inconsiderate asshole."
- **DO remember people's names.** People will be impressed, and they will remember that you remembered. They will then make the effort to remember your name as well. Not many of us make

this extra effort, so you can really separate yourself simply by making it a point to remember people's names.

- **DO get a dog**. It's nice to be surrounded by unconditional love and affection. The dog will also bring a family together.
- **DON'T be afraid to fail**. If you don't allow yourself to try and fail at things, you will never have the joy of having accomplished something that you thought was unattainable.
- **DON'T wait for tomorrow**. Don't ever wait to satisfy an idea, a hope, or a dream. Always take a first step on that idea/hope/dream today. The simplest action on your idea today can be a life changer.
- **DO be competent**. No matter what you do, know your shit!!!!! Competence leads to confidence. Self-confident is where you want to be but never to the point of being an arrogant, pompous prick. Self-confident, yet humble, should be your goal.
- **DON'T allow yourself to become compromised**. Don't allow yourself to owe anyone anything. Don't ask a lot of favors from people. Just do it yourself.
- **Remember**: No matter how bad things are, they can always be worse. You see, the world is a big place and somewhere, someone does have it worse than you. You can use this as a bit of inspiration to pick yourself up and start moving in the right direction. If you've lost a loved one, there is someone in this world who's lost multiple loved ones, and you have

to find a way to be grateful for what you have even in the worst of times.

- **Rejection:** isn't always a bad thing. We all need to be put in our place once in a while. Indeed, rejection leads to humility, and that is a good place to be.
- **Money:** The more you have, the more guarded you have to be. Going through life poor would most definitely suck. But going through life having to guard against everyone and everything for fear of a loss of your money sucks too.
- **DON'T judge.** Chances are that (1) you were not put on this earth to assume the role of judging others, so don't; (2) you don't have all the facts (there are often an assortment of reasons why people are exhibiting behavior that we deem deplorable); (3) you have previously engaged in conduct similar to that which you seek to condemn. If you see someone exhibiting shameful behavior, you may want to just be glad that life hasn't dealt you the same set of cards that is causing this other person to act the way that they are, and move on without comment.
- **DO something!!!!!!!!** There are twenty-four hours in a day. Sleep eight; that leaves you with sixteen hours to accomplish amazing things—to make someone's day, to learn, to teach, to help. Enough with the gadgets and TV and sofa—get going on something productive.
- **DON'T expect much out of others.** They will disappoint you. Yes, this includes family and good

friends. The more you expect of others, the greater the chance they will disappoint you. So, expect less—a lot less—and then when someone rises to the occasion, you will actually be surprised. Better to be surprised than disappointed. If you find yourself disappointed in someone, take some of the blame for having counted on them. It is partially your fault for putting yourself in a position to have to rely on that person.

- **DO stay calm.** Whenever someone is trying to make you angry or upset, the calmer you are, the angrier they will become.

- **Life goes on.** Yes, it does. There are going to be some setbacks, no doubt. But, I have seen the absolute worst things happen to some families (death of a parent/spouse/kid, suicide within a family); at that moment life does seem to stop, and we all mourn for that family and forget about our day-to day trivial nonsense; the community rallies for that one-week period by helping out, etc. but, amazingly, we all go back to our daily routines and the family in mourning is left behind. It's like we are all going 110 mph and when a tragedy strikes, we slow it down to 20 mph and focus on what is important, but soon enough we all start accelerating back to thirty, forty, fifty, and soon enough we're back to our trivial bullshit. We need to find a way to stay at 20 MPH and enjoy what we have because we all take turns being that one family in mourning.

- **DON'T ever think that someone else has it better than you**. Famous people and rich people have their issues as well, so you can't assume that just because they live in a bigger house, have more friends, etc. that somehow they are happier than you.

- **New people/higher-ranking people/famous people**: Many people stumble when introduced to someone new or a person of a "higher" rank, higher position, etc. How do you act? What do you say? Trying to "rise" to someone else's level can backfire. Remember that we all have a few common denominators. We all eat. You can always put everyone at ease with "Hey, where can we get a decent meal around here?" Everyone is now suddenly even. It doesn't matter that person A is a professional athlete and person B is the janitor— they are now even and can talk as equals. So, when you see Justin Beiber or some famous athlete, don't talk to them about their music or their sport, instead, ask them where is the best greasy spoon to grab a bite and nurse a hangover.

- **DON'T take your responsibilities tooooo seriously**. Yes, you want to be a responsible person for sure. But there are problems with becoming too responsible: (1) other people will slack off and piggyback on your extra effort. Make sure everyone has equivalent responsibilities, or else you will be the jackass doing everything; (2) you'll start to think that the world cannot go on without you. If you take your responsibilities too seriously, you will start to miss out on some fun things because you can't do this and you can't do that on account of having these other responsibilities.

- **Define yourself**: Find a few very positive character traits to define yourself. "I am a giving person;" "I am a smart person;" "I am a good friend," whatever. This will allow you to like who you are and shape many of your day-to-day decisions. As the day unfolds and either (1) someone is being a jackass, or (2) there are decisions to be made, you can resort to your core definition and suddenly any perceived drama will just disappear.

- **People who have bad qualties**: They also have good qualities. I've almost lost out on some great friendships on account of looking solely at a person's negative qualities. It is our responsibility to remember that we are not perfect either, and that if people focused only on our negative qualities that we wouldn't be very well-liked either. So, find the good qualities in a person and focus on that. Always try to bring out the best qualities in people, as they will shine. If you're with someone and they are displaying their negative qualities, then take some responsibility for having put them in that position where they have to display their ugly side. You should have put them in a position where they can display their talents. Partially your fault.

- **Being nobody**: is awesome. If you want to become "somebody" (PTA chairperson, big boss, head coach, top dog, whatever) chances are that you may have to step on a few people on your way up. And then, when you finally become "Somebody," you now have a huge target on your back from people who have aspirations of taking what you have. It's a big game out there of people trying to climb the ladder and then pushing other people off. The goal is to get to the top but to be unnoticed.

- **Silence is golden:** I'm just saying. I love silence. Sometimes when we are with others, moments of silence can be awkward. If you ever find yourself in that situation, just let others know that you are totally comfortable not having to hear anybody or anything. Chances are that they will appreciate your candor and find the moments of silence equally satisfying. Then there are others who can't seem to shut up. Hopefully, they have other more positive qualities that override their noise.

- **When you're feeling down/seeking pity:** Boil it down to the most bare-bones essentials. Ask: Do you have your health? Do you have your freedom? If you can answer these two affirmatively, you should be able to pick yourself up. The amazing thing is that people who couldn't answer these questions affirmatively have somehow found ways to pick themselves up and find meaning. That's right, people who have been told that they only have a short time to live or people who have been wrongly imprisoned or held in concentration camps have written about not feeling sorry for themselves and/ or finding dignity in their plight. If these people who are on their deathbed or in a concentration camp can find ways to cope and avoid self-pity, then we are all certainly capable of not allowing the more trivial letdowns (perceived letdowns) bring us down. Find inspiration in these people who have found a way to play the hand that life has dealt them.

- **DON'T battle getting older.** There are some benefits to getting older. You're smarter, have more wisdom, and have a few more bucks in your pocket; hey, that beats making stupid mistakes (again) and struggling. If you constantly battle getting older, you will be unhappy because there isn't any way to beat it.

- **Get up:** Yes, we all need our six-eight hours of sleep and we all need to sit down and take breaks. But if you find yourself on the couch for excessive periods of time watching TV, *get up* and do something. You're more alive when you are vertical. You have an eternity in font of you to be horizontal.

- **It's never too late:**
  - To say you are sorry
  - To admit you are wrong
  - To say thank you
  - To acknowledge someone else's accomplishments

You be the "one": There is always someone within a group who will break out and do something to elevate him or herself above and beyond the status of the group. While everyone else within a group is sort of just wandering aimlessly through a certain segment of life, there is someone who will boldly (1) do something different, or (2) do something more, or (3) just go totally in an opposite direction. This could be as simple as mingling with different groups, volunteering, exercising, networking, and contributing in some way to the community. This person does stuff above and beyond what everyone else in the group is doing. All others in the group will be impressed with and will take inspiration in this person for having the guts and courage to break out and to strive for more. Be this person. Don't just follow what everyone else is doing. You will all get lost together, and one day you'll look up and find that the person who elevated themselves has moved on. Aim to be the person that others are impressed with.

Funerals/wakes: As a society, we need to make a change here. I get it. Someone has died, and we need to find a way that allows all the family and friends to come together to grieve and to mourn. But there is no reason to have the corpse in the same room. That is so messed up. Are we out of our mind to think that the corpse serves a purpose? It's so fucked up and bothersome. I'll say it again. There is no reason to have a corpse in the same room. As a society, can we please agree to remove the corpse from the equation. Please.

Regrets: Oh yes, you are going to have some regrets. I should have, I could have, I wish I didn't, If only I had—Yep, we make mistakes and some prove to be more costly than others. The problem comes when we live in our regrets. *Fuck that*. For every regret we have, we also have many accomplishments. I am so glad I . . ., I have achieved . . . , I can take great pleasure in knowing that I did this . . . and that I didn't do this. *Choose to live in your accomplishments*: It's like I said before, you get to choose your thoughts, so if you find yourself living in your regrets, take a look in the mirror because you now have one more regret—you should be living in your accomplishments, not your regrets.

Be prepared: We all need a little luck. There are some things in life that can be attributed solely to luck—where we are born, who are parents are, the stability and support of the family structure around us, the opportunities that present themselves. To a great extent, anyone reading this book is "lucky" in the sense that they were born in a modernized world and have been given the opportunity to educate themselves to the point of being able to read this book. Yes, that is "lucky" on a certain level. We could have been born into a third-world country with little or no hope of a meaningful and productive life. But here we are having been born into a country that presents us with great opportunities for education, employment, health care, etc. So yes, we are "lucky" indeed. But the absolute key to being "lucky" is having the ability to turn opportunity into success. And the key there is to be prepared.

*Success is where opportunity
meets being well prepared.*

How do you get "well prepared"? It's kind of simple, isn't it? Work your ass off. Go the extra mile. Do more than what is asked of you. Do more. Know more. Opportunities will present themselves, but you have to be prepared in order to turn those opportunities into success. Yes, be grateful for any luck that comes your way. But be prepared so that you can turn opportunities into success. Constantly work on being prepared. Do more. Know more.

Create Your Own Culture: Society is selling us a culture based on status and materialistic possessions. We spend the bulk of our time trying to achieve and obtain more. I suppose we don't want to become stagnant, so we should strive to achieve and obtain more. But more of what? More possessions? A higher rank? Fuck that. But that is what our culture has for sale. Let's try and change that. Change your individual culture so that you strive to achieve and obtain more in other areas, such as community, creativity, friendships, and family. Let's strive to achieve more in these areas; not in materialistic possessions and rank. *Seek to immerse yourself in your community, your family, your friendships, and your creativity, not in your possessions.*

Prejudice: Never think that you are better than anyone solely on account of your race or economic status. Period. You're not. Period. I feel bad for people who are born into a household where hate is allowed to thrive. We must learn and preach tolerance. I'm not saying that this is natural. Indeed, it might be more natural to be prejudiced, so this is something we have to work on and the easiest way is to reread the start of this. *Never think that you are better than anyone solely on account of your race, sex, economic status, or sexual orientation.*

Be aware of your "default setting": Much like electronic products we, too, have "default settings." It is the emotion that we are most comfortable with or the emotion that we revert back to when we are alone. Some of us are "happy," others "optimistic," some "pissed," others "tired." So you see, when we are done with a thought, or a conversation, or a task, whatever, we then revert back to our "default setting," and we probably do so hundreds of times a day. In a big way, our "default setting" kind of shapes us. It would be way too easy to simply say "make your default setting happiness," and move on. I think the lesson has to be this: Be aware of what your default setting is, and if you don't like it, then make the effort to change it. My default setting happens to be anger. I am pissed off and generally pretty comfortable with that. I get irritated kind of quickly, and probably it's an unconscious effort to get to my "happy place" of being pissed off at something or someone. That is my default setting. It's taken a while for me to realize this, but that is my default setting. The key is that I am aware of it and I am okay with it. It kind of gives me an edge. So, do some soul searching. Are you always reverting to being tired? Being happy, optimistic, miserable? Just know what your default setting is, and if it has a negative effect on your life then start to make the conscious and deliberate effort to change it. Fuck you. Sorry, a little bit of my anger slipped out there.

Don't be lame: There will be plenty of time to lie horizontally in a box so until then, make the effort to experience things, enjoy things, teach, interact, volunteer, whatever, get out there and stop making excuses that will only lead you to live a lame life. Let that be the other guy, not you.

"I wish I could be more like": Go ahead and finish that thought. Who did you pick? Someone with a lot of money? Someone with a lot of power? Someone who has achieved great balance? Someone with a solid marriage? How you answered this will tell you a lot about yourself. Hopefully, one day you will be able to answer it this way: There is no one else that I would rather be!!!!! Better yet, others will complete this thought by inserting your name!!! *Wow.* You have become such a solid person that others take inspiration with the way you conduct yourself and the way you live your life.

Emanate positive energy: I've met a few people who seem to somehow light up a room with positive vibes.

I don't know if it is done intentionally. I just know that I can feel it. Look, I am not into that whole Bigfoot, UFO, aliens shit. But I do think that people have the ability to emanate positive energy, and we should all strive to do this. One good trick is to start and finish all communications (e-mails) with positive communication, even if what comes in between isn't so positive. Also, stay away from those who are emanating negative energy. They are toxic. You can feel it, so get away from it. If you somehow feel "stuck" being with this person, take some responsibility for your situation, as you are not "stuck." You have a choice, and you should have chosen not to be with this miserable fuck.

CONCLUSION

Let's wrap this thing up. I think I am repeating myself, or some of the lessons are bleeding into each other.

At the end of the day, you just have to remember to take control of your life. Do not allow yourself to play the part of a helpless victim.

Strive to be a great person. Emanate positive energy in all that you do. Eliminate feelings of hate, jealousy, and resentment and all the negative energy that comes with those feelings. Smile more. Work your ass off. Always have something fun on the horizon. Strive to become such a solid person that others take inspiration with the way you conduct yourself and the way you live your life.

So there it is. It's all in writing. I have now given you all the "life lessons" that I have learned. But I realize that this is just a book, and you may not truly absorb all of the lessons simply by reading the book. I know that the real way to pass all this on to you is for me to *live it*. As I said in the dedication, I really never verbally expressed many or any of these "life lessons," as I wanted you to learn things on your own by observing and by not being manipulated by me or any other adult figure. I vow to live these life lessons in the hope that you observe for yourself how effective or ineffective these lessons are.

I love you both,

Your Father.

(Probably the only time that I have characterized myself as your "father," as this is one of the few times that I have ever assumed that role. You see, one of the things that I have come to learn is that I have been a great "Dad," but not so much of a great "Father." The "Dad" part is kind of easy. It involves being around for you and doing fun stuff together. I'll give myself an A for that "Dad" role. The "Father" part kind of sucks, in that it involves making sure that you have learned some hard-core life lessons. It also involves allowing you to fail and putting you in positions where you might have to struggle. I'm not very good at that. I'll give myself a D on that "Father" role. But hey, I wrote this book so maybe I can squeeze out a C on the Father role. So Dad = A; Father = C; combined score is B and I'll take it.